ODD COUPLES

A Guide to Unlikely
Animal Pairs

BY MARIA BIRMINGHAM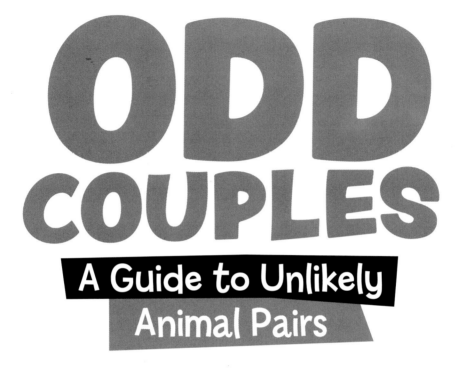

iLLUSTRATED BY RAZ LATiF

OWLKiDS BOOKS

For the entire Owlkids team, because nothing beats pairing up with you on another book – M.B.

To Mylana – R.L.

ACKNOWLEDGMENTS: Much gratitude to my editor, Stacey Roderick, for her enthusiasm, thoughtful edits, and help in shaping this book. My thanks to Raz Latif for his incredible art, as well as to Danielle Arbour for her stellar design work. Many thanks to Doeun Rivendell for offering a helpful eye. And, as always, thanks to Sam and Grace, my favorite pair.

Text © 2023 Maria Birmingham | Illustrations © 2023 Raz Latif

Owlkids Books acknowledges the financial support of the Canada Council for the Arts, the Ontario Arts Council, the Government of Canada through the Canada Book Fund (CBF) and the Government of Ontario through the Ontario Creates Book Initiative for our publishing activities.

Owlkids Books gratefully acknowledges that our office in Toronto is located on the traditional territory of many nations, including the Mississaugas of the Credit, the Chippewa, the Wendat, the Anishinaabeg, and the Haudenosaunee Peoples.

Published in Canada by Owlkids Books Inc., 1 Eglinton Avenue East, Toronto, ON M4P 3A1
Published in the US by Owlkids Books Inc., 1700 Fourth Street, Berkeley, CA 94710

Library of Congress Control Number: 2022950154

Library and Archives Canada Cataloguing in Publication

Title: Odd couples : a guide to unlikely animal pairs / by Maria Birmingham ; illustrated by Raz Latif.
Names: Birmingham, Maria, author. | Latif, Raz, illustrator.
Identifiers: Canadiana 20220470154 | ISBN 9781771475280 (hardcover)
Subjects: LCSH: Animals—Miscellanea—Juvenile literature.
Classification: LCC QL49 .B554 2023 | DDC j590—dc23

Edited by Stacey Roderick | Designed by Danielle Arbour

MIX
Paper | Supporting
responsible forestry
FSC® C008047
www.fsc.org

Manufactured in Shenzhen, Guangdong, China,
in February 2023, by C & C Offset
Job #HW6450

hc   A   B   C   D   E   F

Publisher of Chirp, Chickadee and OWL
www.owlkidsbooks.com | Owlkids Books is a division of bayard canada

Have you ever noticed how some kinds of animals are really hard to tell apart?

Take alligators and crocodiles, for instance. Or leopards and jaguars. And what about frogs and toads? You need to look closely at each of these pairs to figure out exactly who's who!

But there are lots of creatures in the animal kingdom that you'd never confuse with each other. Like giraffes and hummingbirds. Or sharks and snails. They're such different creatures, they couldn't possibly have anything in common. Right? Think again! It turns out these odd couples, and many others, are more alike than meets the eye.

What could this odd couple have in common?

Bee hummingbird

Measures about the size of a bumblebee

Giraffe

Stands tall enough to look into a second-floor window

They **both** hum!

Hummingbirds are so well known for their hum, it's how they got their name. Their fast-beating wings produce the sound you hear. In fact, the bee hummingbird flaps its wings up to 80 times every second when it flies. Besides making that distinctive hum, those super-speedy wings also help hummingbirds do something no other bird can do—fly backward!

Giraffes are also hummers. They can be heard humming away very quietly throughout the night. But scientists aren't sure why. Some think it may be a way for giraffes to communicate with the rest of their herd. Or the humming could simply be a sound that's made as they sleep, similar to how some humans snore.

HUMmmmmmmm Mmmmm

What could this odd couple have in common?

Great white shark

Slices through the sea at top speeds

Snail

Moves s-l-o-w-l-y along
its path of slime

They **both** have a mouth full of teeth!

It's probably no surprise that sharks have lots of teeth. But consider this: great white sharks can have about 300 in their mouth at one time. Most sharks have sharp, triangular teeth that grow in rows. When a tooth breaks off or falls out, one from the row behind moves forward and takes its spot. This happens so often that some sharks can have more than 30,000 teeth over a lifetime!

You might be shocked to find out that a snail has thousands of tiny teeth that cover its tongue. And much like a shark's chompers, snail teeth grow in rows. When a row gets worn down, a new one gradually moves forward to replace it. Instead of chewing the way we do, a snail uses its many teeth to scrape and grind food into very tiny pieces before swallowing it. When it's really quiet, you can even hear this scraping as the snail eats!

What could this odd couple have in common?

Polar bear

Weighs more than two refrigerators

Ussurian tube-nosed bat

Weighs about as much
as a piece of paper

They **both** dig dens in the snow!

Polar bears dig their caves in the snow during the late autumn and winter. While inside these dens, their bodies produce enough heat to keep the caves toasty warm, even when the temperature outside is frigid. Males use their den as a resting place for several days at a time. For females, they're a safe place to give birth to their cubs. They'll nurse and care for their young in the cave for about three months until spring has sprung.

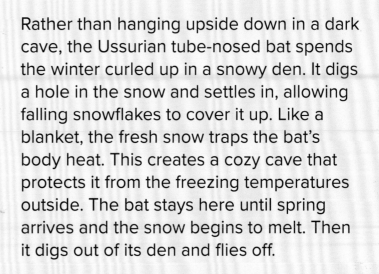

Rather than hanging upside down in a dark cave, the Ussurian tube-nosed bat spends the winter curled up in a snowy den. It digs a hole in the snow and settles in, allowing falling snowflakes to cover it up. Like a blanket, the fresh snow traps the bat's body heat. This creates a cozy cave that protects it from the freezing temperatures outside. The bat stays here until spring arrives and the snow begins to melt. Then it digs out of its den and flies off.

What could this odd couple have in common?

Meerkat

Lives in a system of underground burrows

They **both** snuggle up!

Meerkats live in large groups called mobs. Members of these mobs work together, making sure everyone is well-fed and safe. Meerkats are also quite affectionate. It's not uncommon to see a pair of them standing outside their desert burrow, holding each other in a tight hug. And meerkats often groom one another in the morning sun, using their paws and teeth to clean bugs off their pals.

Believe it or not, honeybees are also snugglers. Worker honeybees form what's called a winter cluster. The whole colony gathers close together in a big group hug around the queen bee. Then they shiver and shake their bodies. This creates heat that keeps the queen cozy. The bees snuggle like this all winter long, switching places occasionally to make sure every member of the colony stays warm.

What could this odd couple have in common?

Wombat

Waddles through the forest on its short legs

Seahorse

Swims through the sea using small
fins near its head to steer

They both have pouches!

Like its kangaroo cousin, a wombat mother carries her baby around in a belly pouch. But rather than the opening being at the top like a kangaroo's, this four-legged creature's pouch opens toward the back of its body. There's a good reason for this. Wombats are big on burrowing and do an awful lot of digging. Having a backward-facing pouch means dirt doesn't end up inside it—and all over baby—as Mom busily digs with her front paws.

A male seahorse has a pouch on its belly, too. The female lays up to 2,000 eggs in this pouch before swimming away. After about four weeks, the eggs hatch. The newborns stay in the pouch a little longer, until they're fully developed. Then the pouch opens, and Dad squeezes the tiny babies out into the sea. The young drift out into the deep blue, caring for themselves from then on.

What could this odd couple have in common?

Peacock

Sleeps in tall forest trees at night

White-tailed deer

Dozes in out-of-the-way spots during the daytime

They **both** use their tail to communicate!

When a male peacock shakes its brightly colored tail, we can hear the rustling sound it makes. But this movement also creates a low, rumbling noise that human ears can't pick up. Other peacocks can hear it, though. The sound tells other males they're getting too close to another peacock's territory. And it lets females, called peahens, know that a male is nearby and looking for a partner.

The white-tailed deer gets its name from the color of the hair underneath its tail. It uses this splash of white to send messages to its young, as well as to other members of its herd. For instance, when a deer senses danger, like an approaching predator, it flees. As it sprints off, the deer raises its tail to show the white patch. This acts like a flag, telling other deer: Follow me and run to safety!

What could this odd couple have in common?

Three-toed sloth

Spends most of its time alone

Kangaroo

Lives in groups of up to 100

They are both strong swimmers!

A sloth spends most of its time hanging around in the treetops of the rain forest, climbing down to the ground to poop once a week. Sometimes a sloth will drop from a branch into water below to make its way to another tree—*sploosh*! While this shaggy creature moves extremely slowly on land, it's much faster in the water, using its long, strong front arms to swim. A sloth can even hold its breath underwater for up to 40 minutes!

On land, a kangaroo uses its powerful back legs to hop at top speed. In the water, it relies on these muscular legs and its short arms to perform its favorite swimming stroke: the doggy paddle! Kangaroos don't swim for fun, though. They will head into the water to flee predators. And any attacker that follows had better watch out. A kangaroo will sometimes use its front paws to hold its enemy underwater.

What could this odd couple have in common?

Opossum

Uses its long tail to help climb trees and cling to branches

Millipede

Uses its many legs
to burrow underground

They **both** protect themselves with stink!

An opossum has a surprising—and smelly—way of getting out of trouble. When it's threatened by a predator, it flops to the ground and lies frozen like a statue. Its eyes stare off into the distance, and its tongue hangs out. And then comes ... the stink! The opossum releases a nasty-smelling goo. After that, a predator usually doesn't stick around. Funnily enough, an opossum doesn't have to try to "play dead." That's just how its body reacts to fear!

You'd think with all those legs, millipedes could escape danger pretty quickly. But it turns out these critters aren't particularly fast. So to protect themselves from enemies, some millipedes rely on a secret weapon. They coil up into a ball and squirt a super-smelly, poisonous liquid from tiny openings along the sides of their body. One whiff of this stench is all it takes to convince most attackers it's time to move along.

What could this odd couple have in common?

Human

Eats a wide variety of foods

Koala

Mainly gobbles up eucalyptus leaves

You both have fingerprints!

You probably notice your fingerprints most when they leave marks on things you handle, such as a drinking glass or device screen. But did you know those swirls and whorls on your fingertips improve your sense of touch? And some experts suggest they may help you grip objects. Your fingerprint pattern is so unique that no one else on Earth has prints that match yours.

Koalas have fingerprints, too. In fact, they're so similar to human prints that even experts have a hard time telling them apart! Koalas likely have fingerprints for the same reason you do—they're helpful for their sense of touch. These creatures are picky eaters and prefer a particular type of leaf. It's thought koalas use their prints to feel leaves to decide which ones they want to crunch on. And every koala has its own specific fingerprint pattern ... just like you do.

Glossary

colony: a group of creatures within a species that live and cooperate with one another

communicate: to share information through actions, sounds, and so on

den: a wild animal's shelter

groom: an activity in which animals clean themselves or others to keep their fur, feathers, or scales healthy

herd: a large group of animals that live together

predator: an animal that hunts other creatures for food

territory: an area of land that one animal or group of animals defends against another